Small Room,
BIG DREAMS

THE JOURNEY OF JULIÁN AND JOAQUIN CASTRO

Written by **Monica Brown**   Illustrated by **Mirelle Ortega**

Quill Tree Books
An Imprint of HarperCollinsPublishers

"WE SHARED A SMALL ROOM AND BIG DREAMS,"

Joaquin Castro said. He looked out at a sea of excited, hopeful faces.

There were millions watching on television, and Joaquin was about to introduce his twin brother, Julián, to the 2012 Democratic National Convention, and to the world. He was filled with love and pride as he said, "I present to you my best friend and my brother, Mayor Julián Castro." The crowd roared with applause as Julián walked out onto the stage.

The Castro brothers' journey didn't begin on a stage, however, but nearly a century earlier, when their grandmother Victoriana crossed the border between Mexico and the United States. Victoriana was born in the middle of the Mexican Revolution, and after both of her parents died, she went north in 1922.

Victoriana was a sad and scared seven-year-old when she held hands with her sister and crossed the border into Texas, to be taken in by relatives they had never met.

Victoriana, who would one day be called Mamo by her grandsons, lived in San Antonio's West Side barrio. Her life was not easy.

Mamo's family was so poor, she had to drop out of school in the third grade to help support them. Though Mamo loved to read, she spent most of her time cleaning houses for five dollars a day in the fancier neighborhoods of north San Antonio. She also cooked and took care of other people's children.

In 1947, Mamo had a daughter of her own, who she named Rosie. As Rosie grew up, she learned that things weren't fair for Mexican Americans in San Antonio. They worked hard but stayed poor, and kids like Rosie weren't allowed to play at certain playgrounds or swim in some public pools.

Rosie graduated from high school at the top of her class and won a scholarship to a local college. Rosie wanted to help her community by becoming a teacher and getting involved in politics.

She was tired of seeing her barrio flood during rainstorms, with trash flowing down the street because of bad drainage systems. Rosie joined the Committee for Barrio Betterment and La Raza Unida Party.

Rosie Castro was the first Chicana to run for San Antonio City Council, in 1971. Rosie came in second and lost, but she still raised her fist, saying, "We will be back!" She knew that one day soon San Antonians would elect leaders who cared about the barrio.

Rosie met a teacher and community volunteer named
Jesse Guzmán, and they had twin sons, first Julián, and then
Joaquin, who was born one minute after his big brother.

Julián and Joaquin looked exactly alike, and they shared a tiny room with their grandmother Mamo, who had moved in to help take care of them. Each night before bed, Mamo Victoriana would sing lullabies in Spanish and say a little prayer for each boy.

"Que Dios los bendiga," Mamo said, praying that her beloved grandsons would be blessed.

They didn't have much money, but Julián and Joaquin loved walking with Mamo to the bookmobile and the library, where they could check out books for free. Mamo had taught herself to read in Spanish and English, and she loved reading to her grandsons.

As the boys grew older, they were always together and always competing—at school, playing sports, and in everything they did. Julián was more studious, and Joaquin was more social, but both loved lucha libre and wrestling with each other! They even argued over their favorite football teams. Julián rooted for the Philadelphia Eagles and Joaquin for the Dallas Cowboys.

They were only eight when their father left, and then it was just Mamo, Rosie, Julián, and Joaquin in the little house in the barrio. Each day, when they came home from school, Mamo would give them milk and cookies. Then it was time for homework. Rosie knew that by studying hard, the boys could reach for the sky. She gave them a dollar for every A they earned on their report card.

After the twins finished their homework, they played in the backyard with their dog, Flea, read wrestling magazines, and explored their neighborhood.

In the summer, Julián and Joaquin would often hop on the bus with their mom, who did social work for the city of San Antonio. The twins climbed trees and played in the grass in the courtyard outside the Plaza de Armas before heading down to Panchito's for a lunch of cheese enchiladas.

When not working, Rosie volunteered on different campaigns to help get more Mexican Americans elected, and she always brought Julián and Joaquin with her. She wanted the boys to learn that participating in their communities through politics was important.

"Work to make people's lives better," Rosie told her sons, and they listened. At home over dinner, they would debate anything from politics to football with their mother.

Julián and Joaquin went to Jefferson High School, where they did great in their classes. The twins played against each other on the tennis team, which usually ended with one of them mad. When their coach saw how competitive they were, she decided to pair them up on a doubles team. Playing side by side, Julián and Joaquin did better than ever and loved sharing their victories!

The brothers pushed each other to do well in school and take more classes. They realized that with night classes and summer school, they could graduate from high school early.

Julián and Joaquin decided to apply to the best colleges in the country, even though few kids in their barrio ever left it. They decided to dream big and both got into Stanford University!

But now they had a new worry. Would it cost too much? Between Rosie's and the twins' hard work, help from the university, and support from their community, Julián and Joaquin made their dreams come true.

Before moving to college, their neighborhood had a party and gifted the boys luggage and sheets and other things they would need to start their college careers. When the time came for Julián and Joaquin to leave Mamo and their mom, they were sad and cried most of the flight from Texas to California.

At Stanford, Julián and Joaquin studied communication and politics. The twins decided to run for spots on the student senate. There were forty-three students competing for ten seats. Instead of competing against each other, Julián and Joaquin worked on the same team, just as they did playing tennis. They tied for first place, each receiving the exact same number of votes. Side by side, the Castro brothers won their first election!

The Castro brothers were happy at Stanford and planning their future when they learned that Mamo was very sick. They flew home to say goodbye to the grandmother who had helped raise them. Even though Mamo was dying, she wanted to hear about their studies.

Mamo couldn't finish her education because she had to go to work cleaning houses, but she was proud that her twin grandsons could! When Mamo passed away, the boys promised to honor their grandmother by using their education to help others.

After college, they went to law school at Harvard University before moving back to San Antonio, where they worked as lawyers and tried to make a difference. Julián and Joaquin didn't want to *wait* for change—they wanted to *work* for change, just like Rosie had taught them, by bringing them to political meetings and demonstrations.

Julián decided to run for office at twenty-six, becoming the youngest person ever elected to the city council. A few years later, he ran for mayor. It was a close race, but he lost.

Luckily, Julián had learned from Mamo and his mom, Rosie, to never give up. A few years later, in 2009, he ran again and won! Now Julián was Mayor Castro. One of the first things he did was put Rosie's old campaign poster up on the wall, to remind him to work hard for his community.

Julián used his new job to fight for prekindergarten education for all the children in his city, not only those who could pay for private schools. He succeeded!

In 2002, Joaquin ran for the Texas House of Representatives and won. At the celebration party, the first thing he did was thank his mom, saying, "We are back!" Joaquin worked to support health care, education, and justice for young people who needed a second chance.

As the Castro brothers' dreams grew bigger, so did their families. Julián met Erica Lira, a teacher who was passionate about education. They married and became parents of a daughter, Carina Victoria, named in memory of Mamo Victoriana, and a son, Cristián.

Joaquin married Anna Flores, and they had a girl, Andrea, and then a boy they named Roman Victor, also honoring his beloved Mamo Victoriana.

One day, after five years of striving to make San Antonio a better place for everyone, Julián received a phone call. It was from the president of the United States, Barack Obama. He asked Julián to serve in his cabinet. Julián said yes.

As secretary of housing and urban development, Julián worked to help people whose communities were destroyed by floods and hurricanes and focused on making sure people of all backgrounds were treated fairly while looking for a home.

Meanwhile, Joaquin decided to run for the United States Congress. He won handily and became Congressman Castro, and he continued his fight for women, for immigrants, and for equality and justice for all. Joaquin joined his brother, Julián, in Washington, DC.

Remembering his trips to the library with Mamo and his mom, Joaquin supported a program that brought books to all children in San Antonio.

Julián and Joaquin Castro are living their dream of working for change.

On January 12, 2019, Julián Castro aimed for his highest dream, announcing his candidacy for president of the United States. His brother, Joaquin, was his campaign chairman. Though Julián wasn't elected president in 2020, he promised to keep fighting for a nation where everyone counts.

We don't know what the future holds, but all will remember the September day in 2012 when Julián Castro stepped onstage at the Democratic National Convention to speak to millions. He had just been introduced by his brother and best friend.

"The days we live in are not easy ones," Julián told the crowd, and then he shared the story of his small room and his big dream, that of people coming together to make this country stronger and more fair.

"It begins now," Julián said, remembering what his Mamo used to say to him and his brother every night. "Que Dios los bendiga. May God bless you, and may God bless the United States of America."

Author's Note

Julián and Joaquin Castro were born on September 16, 1974. Julián is one minute older than his twin. Their story is truly remarkable. They were raised by a tenacious single mother and their beloved grandmother Mamo, who had only a third-grade education. From an early age, Julián and Joaquin were inspired by their mother, Maria del Rosario Castro, known as Rosie. She was a Chicana activist committed to bettering the community and increasing access to the democratic process. She was involved in La Raza Unida, a Chicano nationalist political party that battled social, economic, and political inequality in Mexican American communities. Rosie participated in direct action through protests, marches, and boycotts. She was also a teacher, social worker, and volunteer.

The twins learned about voter registration and political campaigns at an early age, and as they grew and excelled academically and professionally as new lawyers, they soon realized that politics would be their path to meaningful service. The extraordinary thing about the Castro family is that the work Rosie did registering voters and advocating for fair representation before her sons were even born set the groundwork for San Antonio's Latinx population becoming engaged in the political process and electing her talented sons.

Julián Castro served on the city council from 2001 to 2005 and then was elected mayor of San Antonio, serving from 2009 to 2014. He served as President Barack Obama's secretary of housing and urban development from 2014 to 2017. On January 12, 2019, Julián Castro decided to reach for the stars and announced his candidacy for president of the United States. Though he suspended his campaign on January 2, 2020, he continues to be a major progressive political voice.

Joaquin Castro, named after the narrator of Rodolfo "Corky" Gonzales's poem "I Am Joaquin," served as Texas state representative from 2003 to 2013, when he was elected to the United States House of Representatives, serving Texas's Twentieth Congressional District.

Congressman Castro currently serves as the chair of the Congressional Hispanic Caucus in the US House of Representatives and vice chairman of the Foreign Affairs Committee, among other positions.

The journey of the Castro family in the United States is one of working and striving, fighting and dreaming. This book tells the story of Julián, Joaquin, and their passionate vision for the future. Regardless of the outcome of any one political race, the Castro brothers have made an indelible impact on their community, their state, and the United States of America. Of one thing we can be sure: the Castro brothers will keep dreaming.

Glossary

Barrio: A term used to describe a Spanish-speaking neighborhood, often with a high rate of poverty

Chicano/a: An identifier chosen by some Mexican Americans and people of Mexican descent living in the United States and often associated with the Chicano power movement. Chicanx is a more recent iteration, acknowledging the complexities of gender.

La Raza Unida Party: A Chicano nationalist political party founded in the 1970s to increase Chicano/a representation in government. It was active in Texas and California.

Lucha libre: A term used to describe Mexican professional wrestling

Que Dios los bendiga: May God bless you

Sources

Castro, Julián. *An Unlikely Journey: Waking Up from My American Dream*. New York: Little, Brown, 2018.

Fernbach, Erika. *Rosie Castro: Trailblazer*. Self-published, CreateSpace Independent Publishing Platform, 2013.

"Joaquin Castro DNC Speech." September 4, 2012. www.politico.com/story/2012/09/joaquin-castron-dnc-speech-text-080706

Kroll, Andy and *National Journal*. "The Power of Two: Inside the Rise of the Castro Brothers." January 23, 2015. www.theatlantic.com/politics/archive/2015/01/the-power-of-two-inside-the-rise-of-the-castro-brothers/440034/

Merica, Dan. "Julián Castro's CNN Town Hall: Four Takeaways." April 12, 2019. www.cnn.com/2019/04/12/politics/julian-castro-town-hall-takeaways-2020/index.html

Ramshaw, Emily. "The Twin in the Background Takes Center Stage." March 2, 2013. www.nytimes.com/2013/03/03/us/politics/joaquin-castro-the-other-texas-twin-takes-center-stage.html

"Transcript: Julian Castro's DNC Keynote Address." September 4, 2012. www.npr.org/2012/09/04/160574895/transcript-julian-castros-dnc-keynote-address

"Transcript: Julián Castro's Presidential Announcement." January 12, 2019. bnonews.com/index.php/2019/01/transcript-julian-castros-presidential-announcement/

castro.house.gov

"Voices of San Antonio: Rosie Castro," a production of the San Antonio Public Library Foundation. April 3, 2018. Available at https://www.youtube.com/watch?v=iqvhHStukFs&t=7s

For the Dreamers
—M.B.

To Mami
—M.O.

Very special thanks go to Dr. Carmen Tafolla, for her expert feedback.

Quill Tree Books is an imprint of HarperCollins Publishers.

Small Room, Big Dreams: The Journey of Julián and Joaquin Castro
Text copyright © 2021 by Monica Brown
Illustrations copyright © 2021 by Mirelle Ortega
All rights reserved. Manufactured in Italy.
No part of this book may be used or reproduced in any manner whatsoever without written permission except
in the case of brief quotations embodied in critical articles and reviews. For information address HarperCollins
Children's Books, a division of HarperCollins Publishers, 195 Broadway, New York, NY 10007.
www.harpercollinschildrens.com

Library of Congress Control Number: 2020930044
ISBN 978-0-06-298573-6

The artist used Photoshop CC to create the digital illustrations for this book.
Typography by Rachel Zegar   21 22 23 24 25   RTLO   10 9 8 7 6 5 4 3 2 1   ❖   First Edition